MW01519572

THE WORLD OF CRYPTOCURRENCIES

Bitcoin, Blockchain, Ethereum, Smart-Contracts and DeFi

Author:
Jean-Francois Joseph Amyot

Contents

THE WORLD OF CRYPTOCURRENCIES

Bitcoin, Blockchain, Ethereum, Smart-Contracts and DeFi

 ISIN 978-1-387-389575 (paper)

Introduction

The World of Crypto Currencies

The world of cryptocurrency and blockchain technology can be a confusing and intimidating one for those unfamiliar with it. But as the use and adoption of these technologies continues to grow, it is becoming increasingly important for individuals and businesses to understand the basics of how they work.

This book aims to provide a comprehensive introduction to the concepts of bitcoin, blockchain, smart contracts, and crypto exchanges, as well as their potential applications and implications for various industries and society as a whole.

Bitcoin, often referred to as the first and most well-known cryptocurrency, was first introduced in 2009 by an individual or group of individuals known as Satoshi Nakamoto.

Bitcoin is a decentralized digital currency that uses cryptography for security and operates on a peer-to-peer network, meaning that it is not controlled by any central authority or government.

Instead, transactions are verified and recorded on a public, distributed ledger known as the blockchain.

The blockchain is the underlying technology that powers bitcoin and other cryptocurrencies. It is a decentralized and distributed database that records transactions on multiple computers, or "nodes," simultaneously. This means that the data is not stored in a single location and is instead spread out across the network.

The decentralized nature of the blockchain makes it resistant to tampering or fraud, as any changes to the data must be approved by a majority of the nodes in the network.

Smart contracts, another important concept in the world of blockchain and cryptocurrency, are self-executing contracts with the terms of the agreement between buyer and seller being directly written into lines of code.

These contracts are stored on the blockchain and are automatically enforced when certain conditions are met. This means that they can facilitate the exchange of money, property, or anything of value in a transparent and secure manner without the need for intermediaries.

Crypto exchanges, also known as digital currency exchanges, are online platforms where users can buy, sell, and trade cryptocurrencies. These exchanges act as intermediaries between buyers and sellers, facilitating the exchange of cryptocurrencies for fiat money or other cryptocurrencies.

There are many different types of crypto exchanges, each with its own unique features and fees.

In this book, we will delve deeper into the concepts of bitcoin, blockchain, smart contracts, and crypto exchanges, exploring their potential applications and implications for various industries and society as a whole.

We will also discuss the challenges and opportunities presented by these technologies, as well as the potential risks and benefits for individuals and businesses considering using or investing in them.

Throughout the book, we will provide examples and case studies to illustrate the practical applications of these technologies and help readers understand how they work in the real world.

We will also address common misconceptions and provide resources for further learning and exploration.

By the end of this book, readers should have a solid understanding of the basics of bitcoin, blockchain, smart contracts, and crypto exchanges, as well as the potential impact these technologies may have on various industries and society as a whole.

Whether you are a beginner looking to learn more about these technologies or an experienced professional looking to expand your knowledge, this book aims to provide a comprehensive and accessible introduction to the world of cryptocurrency and blockchain technology.

"The future of money is digital currency."

- Bill Gates

Chapter 1

The History of Bitcoin: From Cryptocurrency to Global Movement

Bitcoin is a decentralized digital currency that was created in 2009 by an unknown individual or group of individuals using the pseudonym Satoshi Nakamoto.

It was the first cryptocurrency to be successfully implemented, and it has since spawned a whole industry of cryptocurrencies that use similar technologies.

The idea for Bitcoin arose in the aftermath of the global financial crisis of 2007-2008, which highlighted the need for a more secure and transparent financial system. Nakamoto believed that the traditional financial system, which is based on central banks and intermediaries, was prone to fraud and abuse.

He proposed a new system that would be based on cryptographic techniques and distributed ledger technology, which would allow for peer-to-peer transactions without the need for a central authority.

The key technological innovation behind Bitcoin is the blockchain, which is a decentralized ledger that records all transactions on the network. The blockchain is maintained by a network of computers, or nodes, that work together to verify and validate transactions. Once a transaction is verified, it is added to the blockchain and becomes part of a permanent record.

This makes it extremely difficult to alter or forge transactions, as any attempt to do so would require the consensus of the entire network.

Bitcoin was initially met with skepticism and faced numerous challenges. One of the main criticisms was that it was vulnerable to attacks and could be used for illegal activities, such as money laundering or drug trafficking.

Despite these challenges, Bitcoin slowly gained traction and began to be accepted by a small but growing number of merchants and individuals.

One of the key events in the history of Bitcoin was the collapse of the Mt. Gox exchange in 2014, which was one of the largest Bitcoin exchanges at the time.

The collapse was caused by a combination of hacking and mismanagement, and it resulted in the loss of hundreds of millions of dollars' worth of Bitcoin. Despite the setback, Bitcoin continued to grow and gain mainstream acceptance.

Today, Bitcoin is widely recognized as a legitimate financial asset and is traded on a number of exchanges around the world. It has also spawned a whole industry of blockchain-based technologies, including smart contracts and decentralized applications, which have the potential to disrupt a wide range of industries.

While Bitcoin has faced numerous challenges and controversies over the years, it has also inspired a global movement of individuals and organizations who believe in the potential of decentralized technologies to create a more open, transparent, and secure financial system.

This movement includes developers, entrepreneurs, investors, and activists who are working to advance the adoption and development of cryptocurrencies and blockchain technologies.

In conclusion, Bitcoin has come a long way since its inception in 2009. From a small and obscure cryptocurrency, it has evolved into a global movement that is driving innovation and disruption in the financial industry. While its future is uncertain, there is no doubt that Bitcoin has made a lasting impact and will continue to shape the way we think about money and financial systems in the years to come.

"Cryptocurrency represents the biggest transfer of wealth our generation has ever seen. Don't miss out on this opportunity."

- Tim Draper

Chapter 2

Understanding Blockchain Technology: The
Basics of Distributed Ledgers

Blockchain technology is a decentralized
and distributed digital ledger that is used to record
transactions on multiple computers so that the
record cannot be altered retroactively without the
alteration of all subsequent blocks and the
consensus of the network. In other words, it is a
type of database that is shared and maintained by
a network of computers, rather than being
controlled by a single entity.

The concept of a distributed ledger dates
back to the early 1990s, but it was not until the
creation of Bitcoin in 2009 that it was fully
realized as a practical technology.

Bitcoin was the first successful
implementation of a decentralized and distributed
ledger, and it used blockchain technology to record
and verify transactions on its network.

The key feature of a blockchain is that it
allows multiple parties to reach consensus on a

single version of a record without the need for a central authority. This is achieved through the use of cryptographic techniques, which ensure the integrity and security of the data on the blockchain.

One of the main benefits of blockchain technology is its ability to facilitate secure and transparent peer-to-peer transactions. Because the ledger is decentralized and distributed, there is no central point of control, which makes it much more difficult for fraud or tampering to occur.

Additionally, the transparency of the blockchain allows for increased accountability and trust between parties, as all transactions are recorded and publicly available for anyone to see.

Blockchains can be either public or private, depending on the level of access and control. Public blockchains, such as the Bitcoin blockchain, are open to anyone and are maintained by a network of volunteers. Private blockchains, on the other hand, are restricted to a specific group of individuals or organizations and are typically used for internal applications, such as supply chain management or financial record keeping.

One of the main challenges of blockchain technology is scalability. Because all transactions must be verified by the entire network, the number of transactions that can be processed per second is limited. This has led to the development of various scaling solutions, such as the Lightning Network for Bitcoin, which aims to increase the speed and efficiency of transactions.

In addition to cryptocurrencies, blockchain technology has a wide range of potential applications in various industries. Some examples include supply chain management, where it can be used to track the movement of goods and materials; voting systems, where it can provide a secure and transparent way to cast and count votes; and real estate, where it can be used to record and verify property ownership.

There are also numerous startups and organizations that are exploring the use of blockchain technology for social impact initiatives, such as increasing transparency and accountability in the charitable sector or enabling peer-to-peer energy trading.

In conclusion, blockchain technology is a revolutionary innovation that has the potential to disrupt and transform a wide range of industries. It offers a secure and transparent way for parties to reach consensus on a single version of a record, and it has the potential to enable more efficient and secure transactions. While there are still challenges to be addressed, such as scalability and regulatory issues, the future of blockchain technology is bright and holds great promise for a wide range of applications.

"Cryptocurrencies have the potential to radically transform our economy and the way we think about money."

- Charles Lee, creator of Litecoin

Chapter 3

Exploring Ethereum: Smart Contracts and
Decentralized Applications

Ethereum is a decentralized, open-source blockchain platform that enables the creation of smart contracts and decentralized applications (dApps).

It was created in 2015 by Vitalik Buterin, a Russian-Canadian programmer, and has since become one of the most popular platforms for building and deploying dApps.

Smart contracts are self-executing contracts with the terms of the agreement between buyer and seller being directly written into lines of code. The code and the agreements contained therein are stored and replicated on the blockchain network. Smart contracts allow for the automation of processes, reducing the need for intermediaries and increasing the speed and efficiency of transactions.

Decentralized applications, or dApps, are applications that run on a decentralized network and are not controlled by any single entity. They are built on top of blockchain technology and use smart contracts to facilitate the exchange of information and value.

dApps have the potential to disrupt a variety of industries, including finance, real estate, and voting systems.

One of the main advantages of Ethereum is its use of smart contracts, which enable secure and transparent transactions without the need for intermediaries. This not only reduces the risk of fraud but also reduces the cost of transactions, as intermediaries can be expensive.

Ethereum also has a large and active developer community, which has contributed to the creation of a wide range of dApps. These dApps include decentralized exchanges, prediction markets, and gaming platforms, to name a few.

One of the most well-known dApps built on Ethereum is CryptoKitties, a virtual pet game that allows players to buy, sell, and breed virtual cats. Each cat is represented by a unique digital asset stored on the Ethereum blockchain, and the ownership of the asset is recorded on the blockchain as well.

Another popular dApp built on Ethereum is Augur, a decentralized prediction market platform that allows users to create and trade on the outcomes of real-world events. Augur uses smart contracts to facilitate the creation and settlement of markets, and all transactions are recorded on the blockchain, providing a level of transparency and security not possible with traditional prediction markets.

In addition to its use in dApps, Ethereum is also being explored for use in a variety of other applications, such as supply chain management and identity verification. For example, a company could use Ethereum to track the movement of goods through the supply chain, ensuring that all parties involved in the transaction have access to accurate and up-to-date information.

Ethereum has the potential to revolutionize the way we conduct transactions and interact with each other online. Its use of smart contracts and decentralized applications allows for greater security, transparency, and efficiency, and its active developer community means that it is constantly evolving and improving. As more and more people become aware of the benefits of Ethereum, it is likely that we will see it being used in an increasingly diverse range of applications in the future.

"Cryptocurrencies are a natural next step in the evolution of money."

- Erik Voorhees, CEO of ShapeShift

Chapter 4

The Rise of DeFi: Decentralized Finance and its Potential Impact

Decentralized finance, or DeFi for short, has emerged as a major trend in the cryptocurrency and blockchain space in recent years.

DeFi refers to a new financial system that is built on top of blockchain technology, with the goal of providing a more open, transparent, and secure alternative to traditional financial services.

One of the main drivers behind the rise of DeFi is the increasing popularity of cryptocurrencies, such as Bitcoin and Ethereum. These digital assets have gained widespread adoption in recent years, and have been embraced by a growing number of individuals and institutions as a legitimate form of currency and investment.

However, traditional financial services have not always been able to keep up with the rapid pace of innovation in the cryptocurrency space.

Many traditional banks and financial institutions are still slow to adopt new technologies, and are often hesitant to support cryptocurrency transactions due to concerns over security and regulatory compliance.

This has led to a gap in the market, which DeFi has been able to fill by offering a range of financial services that are built on top of blockchain technology. These services include decentralized exchanges (DEXs), which allow users to buy and sell cryptocurrencies without the need for a central authority, as well as decentralized lending and borrowing platforms, which allow users to lend and borrow money using cryptocurrency as collateral.

DeFi also includes a range of other financial services, such as stablecoins (cryptocurrencies that are pegged to the value of a traditional asset, such as the US dollar), prediction markets, and insurance platforms. These services are designed to be more transparent, secure, and accessible than traditional financial services, and are often able to offer more competitive rates and fees as well.

The rise of DeFi has been driven by several key factors. One of the main drivers has been the increasing adoption of blockchain technology, which has made it possible to build decentralized financial services that are secure, transparent, and resistant to fraud.

Another factor has been the growing popularity of cryptocurrency and the increasing demand for alternative financial services. As more and more people have become interested in investing in and using cryptocurrency, there has been a corresponding increase in the demand for financial services that are built on top of blockchain technology.

Finally, the rise of DeFi has also been driven by the increasing regulatory scrutiny of traditional financial services, which has led many people to seek out alternative financial options that are outside the traditional financial system.

The potential impact of DeFi is significant, as it has the potential to disrupt traditional financial services and transform the way that financial transactions are conducted. DeFi could potentially lead to a more inclusive and democratized financial system, one that is more accessible to people in all parts of the world, and that is more transparent and secure.

DeFi could also have a major impact on the global economy, as it has the potential to change the way that money is created, circulated, and invested. With DeFi, it is possible to create new forms of currency and financial instruments that are not controlled by traditional financial institutions, which could potentially lead to a more decentralized and stable global financial system.

Overall, the rise of DeFi represents a major shift in the financial landscape, and it is likely to have a significant impact on the way that financial transactions are conducted in the future. While there are still many challenges and obstacles to overcome, the potential benefits of DeFi are significant, and it is likely to continue to grow and evolve in the coming years.

"Cryptocurrencies have the ability to not only disrupt the payment industry, but also the monetary system as a whole."

- Tyler Winklevoss, co-founder of Gemini

Chapter 5

Web3 and the Future of the Internet:
Decentralization and Interoperability

The internet as we know it today is dominated by a few large tech companies that control much of the infrastructure, data, and user experience. This centralization has led to a number of problems, including data breaches, censorship, and the concentration of power and wealth in the hands of a few.

Web3 technologies, also known as decentralized technologies or blockchain technologies, offer a solution to these problems by decentralizing the internet and enabling greater interoperability between different systems and platforms.

Decentralization refers to the distribution of power and control across a network rather than having it concentrated in a single entity. In the context of the internet, decentralization means that there is no single point of control or failure and that users have more control over their own data and online experiences.

Blockchain technology is a key component of Web3 technologies and is essentially a decentralized, distributed ledger that allows for secure and transparent record-keeping. It allows for the creation of decentralized applications (dApps) and decentralized autonomous organizations (DAOs) that operate on a decentralized network rather than a single centralized server.

One major benefit of decentralization is that it reduces the risk of data breaches and censorship. Because there is no central point of control, it is much harder for hackers to gain access to sensitive data or for governments to censor certain content. This is especially important in countries with authoritarian governments that have a history of censoring or controlling the internet.

Interoperability, on the other hand, refers to the ability of different systems and platforms to work together and exchange information seamlessly. In the context of the internet, interoperability means that different platforms and protocols can communicate with each other and share data without the need for intermediate layers or gatekeepers.

Web3 technologies enable greater interoperability by allowing for the creation of decentralized protocols and standards that can be used by different platforms and systems. This allows for the creation of a more open and interconnected internet, where users can move freely between different platforms and networks without having to worry about compatibility issues.

One example of a Web3 technology that is helping to increase interoperability is the Interledger Protocol (ILP), which allows for the exchange of value across different ledgers and networks. This is important because it allows for the creation of a more inclusive and accessible financial system that is not tied to any specific platform or currency.

Another example is the Interplanetary File System (IPFS), which is a decentralized protocol for sharing and storing files. It allows users to access and share content without having to rely on a central server or storage provider, and it also enables greater interoperability between different platforms and networks.

Overall, Web3 technologies have the potential to significantly transform the internet and the way we use it. Decentralization and interoperability are key components of this transformation, and they offer a number of benefits such as increased security, privacy, and accessibility.

As Web3 technologies continue to mature and gain wider adoption, we can expect to see a more decentralized and interoperable internet that is more resistant to censorship and more inclusive for all users. This will have far-reaching implications for industries such as finance, education, healthcare, and more, and it has the potential to create a more equitable and democratic online environment.

"Cryptocurrency is the future of money, and it's here to stay."

- Brian Armstrong, CEO of Coinbase

Chapter 6

Bitcoin and the Financial Industry: Disrupting Traditional Models

Bitcoin is a decentralized digital currency that was created in 2009 by an unknown individual or group of individuals under the pseudonym Satoshi Nakamoto. It is based on a decentralized ledger technology called the blockchain, which allows it to be transferred from one person to another without the need for intermediaries like banks. This peer-to-peer nature of bitcoin has made it a popular choice for individuals and businesses looking for an alternative to traditional financial systems.

Since its inception, bitcoin has been hailed as a disruptor to traditional financial models. Its decentralized nature and lack of ties to any particular country or government make it a potentially disruptive force in the financial industry. The ability to transfer value directly between individuals without the need for intermediaries has the potential to revolutionize the way we think about and use money.

One of the main ways in which bitcoin is disrupting traditional financial models is through its use as a digital asset. Unlike traditional currencies, which are backed by governments and central banks, bitcoin is not backed by any central authority. Instead, its value is determined by market forces, such as supply and demand. This has made it a popular investment vehicle for those looking to diversify their portfolios and hedge against traditional financial instruments.

Another way in which bitcoin is disrupting traditional financial models is through its use as a medium of exchange. Because it is decentralized and not tied to any particular country or government, bitcoin can be used to make international transactions without the need for intermediaries like banks or credit card companies. This can be especially useful for individuals or businesses in countries with unstable economies or high levels of inflation, as it allows them to transfer value without being subject to the same risks as traditional currencies.

Bitcoin is also disrupting traditional financial models through its use as a store of value. While traditional currencies can lose value over time due to inflation or other economic factors, bitcoin is resistant to these types of changes because its supply is limited. This makes it an attractive option for those looking to preserve the value of their wealth over time.

Despite the potential for disruption, bitcoin and other cryptocurrencies have faced significant challenges in the financial industry. One of the main issues has been their volatility, which has made them difficult to use as a stable store of value.

Additionally, there have been concerns about the lack of regulation in the cryptocurrency market, which has led to instances of fraud and financial crimes.

Despite these challenges, bitcoin and other cryptocurrencies are gaining traction in the financial industry. Many major financial institutions, such as banks and investment firms, have begun exploring the use of bitcoin and blockchain technology in their operations. This includes the use of bitcoin for international transactions, as well as the development of new financial products based on blockchain technology.

Overall, it is clear that bitcoin and other cryptocurrencies have the potential to disrupt traditional financial models in a number of ways. While there are still challenges to be addressed, the increasing adoption of bitcoin and blockchain technology by major financial institutions suggests that these technologies are here to stay.

As more people and businesses begin using bitcoin and other cryptocurrencies, it is likely that we will see a greater impact on traditional financial models and the way we think about money.

"The decentralized nature of cryptocurrency means that it can't be controlled by any government, bank, or corporation."

- Vitalik Buterin, co-founder of Ethereum

Chapter 7

Blockchain in Supply Management: Enhancing
Transparency and Efficiency

Blockchain technology has the potential to revolutionize supply chain management by enhancing transparency and efficiency.

Supply chains are complex systems that involve the movement of goods and services from raw materials to the end consumer. These systems often span multiple countries and involve numerous stakeholders, including suppliers, manufacturers, wholesalers, retailers, and logistics providers. As a result, it can be challenging to track the flow of goods and information within the supply chain, which can lead to inefficiencies and a lack of transparency.

One of the key benefits of blockchain in supply chain management is the ability to create a transparent, immutable record of transactions. A blockchain is a decentralized, distributed ledger that records transactions in a secure, chronological, and transparent manner. Each transaction is recorded as a block, which is linked to the previous block in the chain. This creates a tamper-evident record that cannot be altered without leaving a trace.

In the context of supply chain management, a blockchain can be used to track the movement of goods from the point of origin to the point of consumption. This can include tracking the movement of raw materials, intermediate products, and finished goods.

Each stakeholder in the supply chain can add information to the blockchain, such as the location, quantity, and quality of the goods being transported. This creates a single source of truth that can be accessed by all stakeholders, enabling them to track the movement of goods in real-time. Another benefit of blockchain in supply chain management is the ability to improve efficiency by automating certain processes.

For example, smart contracts can be used to automate the execution of complex business logic, such as the release of payment when certain conditions are met. This can help to reduce the need for manual processes, which can be time-consuming and prone to errors.

In addition, blockchain technology can help to improve the traceability of goods within the supply chain. This is particularly important in industries where the traceability of goods is critical, such as the food and pharmaceutical industries.

By using blockchain to track the movement of goods, it is possible to quickly and easily trace the origin and movement of a product in the event of a recall or contamination.

One potential use case for blockchain in supply chain management is in the tracking of the movement of goods across international borders. International trade is a complex process that involves numerous stakeholders, including customs officials, carriers, and regulatory agencies. By using a blockchain to track the movement of goods, it is possible to create a single source of truth that can be accessed by all stakeholders. This can help to streamline the customs process and reduce the risk of fraud and errors.

There are also a number of potential applications for blockchain in the logistics industry. For example, a blockchain could be used to track the movement of cargo and shipments, allowing logistics providers to optimize routes and improve delivery times. In addition, a blockchain could be used to track the maintenance and repairs of vehicles and equipment, helping to improve the efficiency and reliability of the logistics network.

Overall, blockchain technology has the potential to significantly enhance transparency and efficiency within the supply chain. By creating a transparent, immutable record of transactions, automating certain processes, and improving traceability, blockchain can help to streamline the supply chain and create a more efficient and effective system. While there are still challenges to be overcome, such as the need for standardization and the integration of legacy systems, the benefits of blockchain in supply chain management are clear and are likely to become increasingly important as the technology continues to mature.

"Cryptocurrency is not just a fad, it's a revolution. It has the potential to change the way we think about and use money."

- Roger Ver, CEO of Bitcoin.com

Chapter 8

The Role of Ethereum in Identity Management
and Digital Ownership

Ethereum is a decentralized, open-source blockchain platform that enables the creation of smart contracts and decentralized applications (dApps). One of the key areas where Ethereum has the potential to have a significant impact is in the realm of identity management and digital ownership.

Identity management refers to the process of verifying and authenticating the identity of individuals or entities, as well as managing and storing identity-related information. Digital ownership, on the other hand, refers to the concept of owning and controlling digital assets or data. Both of these areas have traditionally been reliant on centralized systems, which can be vulnerable to security breaches, fraud, and other types of abuse.

Ethereum, with its decentralized and immutable nature, has the potential to revolutionize the way we think about identity management and digital ownership. We will explore the various ways in which Ethereum can be used to facilitate these processes, as well as the potential benefits and challenges associated with this technology.

One of the key features of Ethereum is the ability to create and execute smart contracts. A smart contract is a self-executing contract with the terms of the agreement between buyer and seller being directly written into lines of code. The code and the agreements contained therein are stored on the Ethereum blockchain, which is a decentralized, transparent, and immutable ledger.

Smart contracts can be used to facilitate the verification and authentication of identity-related information. For example, an individual could create a smart contract that verifies their identity through the use of a government-issued ID, such as a driver's license or passport. The smart contract could then be used to authenticate the individual's identity whenever they need to access a particular service or asset.

Smart contracts can also be used to facilitate the management and storage of identity-related information. For example, an individual could create a smart contract that stores their personal information, such as their name, address, and date of birth. This information could then be accessed by other parties, such as financial institutions or government agencies, in a secure and transparent manner.

In addition to facilitating the verification and authentication of identity, Ethereum can also be used to enable digital ownership. One of the key challenges with digital ownership is the lack of a clear and secure way to establish and transfer ownership of digital assets. Ethereum can help to solve this problem through the use of non-fungible tokens (NFTs).

NFTs are unique digital assets that are stored on the Ethereum blockchain. They can represent a wide range of digital assets, such as artwork, music, videos, and even virtual real estate. NFTs are unique in that they cannot be exchanged for other assets on a one-to-one basis, as they are considered to be non-fungible.

The use of NFTs can help to establish clear ownership of digital assets and facilitate the transfer of ownership in a secure and transparent manner. For example, an artist could create an NFT of their artwork and sell it to a collector. The

NFT would represent ownership of the artwork and the transaction could be recorded on the Ethereum blockchain, providing a clear record of ownership.

In addition to facilitating the ownership of digital assets, Ethereum can also be used to enable the creation of decentralized autonomous organizations (DAOs). A DAO is a decentralized organization that is governed by a set of rules encoded into a smart contract. Members of a DAO can make decisions about the direction of the organization through the use of voting rights, which are typically based on the number of tokens held by the member.

DAOs have the potential to disrupt traditional organizational structures by enabling decentralized decision-making and allowing for the creation of organizations that are not bound by geography or traditional power dynamics.

"Cryptocurrency allows for greater financial inclusion, as it enables individuals and organizations to easily send and receive payments without the need for traditional intermediaries."

- Brad Garlinghouse, CEO of Ripple

Chapter 9

DeFi and Inclusive Financial Systems:
Opportunities for Emerging Markets

Decentralized finance, or DeFi for short, has been gaining increasing attention in recent years as a way to offer more inclusive financial services to people in emerging markets.

DeFi is a financial system built on blockchain technology that allows for peer-to-peer transactions and financial services without the need for traditional intermediaries such as banks. This decentralized approach has the potential to provide financial services to underserved and unbanked populations in emerging markets who may not have access to traditional financial institutions.

One of the main benefits of DeFi is that it can be accessed by anyone with an internet connection. This is especially important in emerging markets where traditional financial infrastructure may be limited or non-existent.

DeFi platforms can be accessed via a smartphone or other device, allowing people to access financial services even if they do not have a bank account or live in a remote area.

Another advantage of DeFi is that it can offer financial services at a lower cost than traditional financial institutions. This is because DeFi platforms are decentralized and do not have the same overhead costs as traditional financial institutions. This means that DeFi can offer financial services at a lower cost to consumers, making it more accessible to those in emerging markets who may not have the means to afford traditional financial services.

DeFi also has the potential to offer more innovative financial products and services. For example, DeFi platforms can offer decentralized stablecoins, which are digital assets pegged to the value of a traditional asset such as a currency or commodity. This can provide a stable store of value for people in emerging markets who may not have access to stable currencies.

DeFi platforms can also offer decentralized exchanges, which allow for the buying and selling of assets without the need for a central authority.

This can provide more opportunities for people in emerging markets to participate in the global financial system.

However, DeFi also has some limitations and challenges that need to be addressed in order to fully realize its potential for inclusive financial systems in emerging markets.

One challenge is the issue of scalability. DeFi platforms are built on blockchain technology, which can have limited capacity and slow transaction speeds compared to traditional financial systems. This can make it difficult for DeFi platforms to handle large volumes of transactions, which may limit their ability to serve a large number of users.

Another challenge is the issue of regulation. DeFi platforms operate outside of traditional financial systems and are not subject to the same regulatory frameworks as traditional financial institutions. This can make it difficult for regulators to oversee and protect consumers using DeFi platforms.

In addition, DeFi platforms may not have the same level of security as traditional financial institutions, which can make them vulnerable to cyber-attacks and other forms of fraud.

Despite these challenges, DeFi has the potential to revolutionize financial systems in emerging markets and provide more inclusive financial services to underserved populations.

To fully realize this potential, it will be important for DeFi platforms to address scalability and regulatory issues, as well as work to improve security and protect consumers. In addition, it will be important for DeFi platforms to partner with traditional financial institutions and regulators in order to bring DeFi to a wider audience and ensure that it is used in a responsible and sustainable manner.

Overall, DeFi has the potential to revolutionize financial systems in emerging markets and provide more inclusive financial services to underserved populations. While there are challenges that need to be addressed in order to fully realize this potential, DeFi has the potential to bring about significant positive changes in the way financial services are provided in emerging markets. As such, it is an exciting and promising area of development that is worth watching closely in the coming years.

"Cryptocurrency is a game-changer. It allows people to take control of their own financial future and be their own bank."

- Roger Keith, co-founder of Uphold

Chapter 10

Web3 and the Future of Online Privacy Data Management

The concept of web3, or the third generation of the World Wide Web, refers to the integration of blockchain technology into the internet.

This integration is expected to bring about significant changes to the way we use and interact with the internet, including an increased focus on online privacy. In this chapter, we will explore how decentralized data management, a key aspect of web3, is set to revolutionize the way we think about online privacy.

One of the main goals of web3 is to create a decentralized internet that is not controlled by a single entity or group. This decentralized structure is made possible through the use of blockchain technology, which allows for the creation of distributed networks where data is stored and validated by multiple parties rather than being stored on a centralized server. This decentralized approach to data management has the potential to significantly improve online privacy by reducing the risk of data breaches and eliminating the need for users to trust a single entity with their personal information.

One of the key benefits of decentralized data management is that it allows users to have more control over their personal information. With traditional centralized data management systems, users are often required to hand over their personal information to a third party in order to access certain services or content. This can leave them vulnerable to data breaches, as a single point of failure in the system can compromise the security of all the data stored within it.

In contrast, decentralized data management systems allow users to store their personal information on their own devices or in decentralized storage systems, such as the InterPlanetary File System (IPFS).

This means that users can retain control over their data and decide for themselves how and when it is shared.

Another advantage of decentralized data management is that it can help to reduce the risk of data misuse. With centralized systems, it is often difficult for users to know how their data is being used or shared, as the data is stored and managed by a third party. This lack of transparency can lead to situations where data is misused or sold without the user's knowledge or consent.

In contrast, decentralized data management systems use smart contracts to define the terms under which data can be accessed and used. These contracts are stored on the blockchain, making them transparent and tamper-proof. This means that users can have greater confidence in the way their data is being used, as they can see exactly how it is being shared and under what conditions.

Decentralized data management also has the potential to improve online privacy by reducing the risk of censorship. In centralized systems, a single entity has control over the data that is stored and accessed, which means that they also have the ability to censor certain types of content or block access to certain services.

In decentralized systems, censorship is much more difficult as the data is distributed across a network of computers, making it much harder for any one entity to control or manipulate.

This can help to create a more open and free internet, where users have greater control over what they see and access.

Overall, decentralized data management is set to play a key role in the future of online privacy. By allowing users to have greater control over their personal information and reducing the risk of data breaches, misuse, and censorship, it has the potential to create a more secure and transparent internet that puts the user's privacy first.

"Cryptocurrency is the first native digital medium for value. It's a huge deal."

- Wences Casares, CEO of Xapo

Chapter 11

Bitcoin, Blockchain, and the Environment:
Sustainability and Energy

Bitcoin is a decentralized digital currency that utilizes blockchain technology to facilitate secure and transparent transactions.

One of the primary criticisms of Bitcoin and blockchain technology is their potential impact on the environment. The mining process, which is necessary to create new bitcoins and verify transactions on the blockchain, requires significant amounts of energy and has been linked to an increase in carbon emissions.

In this chapter, we will explore the sustainability of Bitcoin and the environmental impact of blockchain technology, as well as potential solutions to address these issues: Energy Consumption and Carbon Emissions.

The mining process for Bitcoin involves the use of specialized computers, known as miners, to solve complex mathematical equations. These equations serve to verify transactions on the blockchain, and miners are rewarded with a small amount of Bitcoin for their efforts.

The energy consumption of Bitcoin mining has been a source of concern, as the process requires a significant amount of electricity. According to a study published in the journal Joule, Bitcoin mining consumes about the same amount of energy as the entire country of Switzerland. This energy consumption is largely driven by the use of specialized hardware, which requires a constant supply of electricity to function.

The high energy consumption of Bitcoin mining has also been linked to an increase in carbon emissions. The electricity used to power the miners is often generated from fossil fuels, such as coal and natural gas, which are major sources of greenhouse gases. This means that the production of Bitcoin can contribute to climate change through the emission of carbon dioxide and other greenhouse gases.

Potential Solutions:

There are a number of potential solutions to address the energy consumption and carbon emissions associated with Bitcoin and blockchain technology.

One solution is to shift to renewable energy sources. Many Bitcoin mining operations are located in regions with access to cheap, renewable energy, such as hydroelectric or geothermal power. By utilizing these sources of energy, mining operations can significantly reduce their carbon footprint.

Another solution is to increase the efficiency of mining hardware. The use of specialized hardware is a major contributor to the energy consumption of Bitcoin mining, so improving the efficiency of these devices could significantly reduce energy usage.

There are also a number of alternative blockchain technologies that have been developed with a focus on sustainability. For example, Ethereum is a blockchain platform that uses a proof-of-stake consensus algorithm, which requires significantly less energy than the proof-of-work algorithm used by Bitcoin. Other alternatives, such as EOS and TRON, also use proof-of-stake algorithms and have a lower energy consumption than Bitcoin.

Finally, the use of Bitcoin and blockchain technology can be limited to reduce their overall impact on the environment. While Bitcoin and other cryptocurrencies have gained widespread adoption, they still represent a small portion of the global financial system. Limiting the use of Bitcoin and other cryptocurrencies could significantly reduce their energy consumption and carbon emissions.

Bitcoin and blockchain technology have the potential to revolutionize the financial industry, but they also have the potential to impact the environment. The energy consumption and carbon emissions associated with Bitcoin mining have raised concerns about the sustainability of these technologies.

However, there are a number of potential solutions that can address these issues, including the use of renewable energy sources, the improvement of mining hardware efficiency, and the adoption of alternative blockchain technologies with a focus on sustainability. By considering these solutions, it may be possible to mitigate the environmental impact of Bitcoin and blockchain technology and ensure their long-term sustainability.

"Cryptocurrency allows for fast and cheap transactions, which is particularly useful for cross-border payments."

- Balaji Srinivasan, CEO of 21.co

Chapter 12

The Potential of Bitcoin, Blockchain, Ethereum, Defi and Web3: Imagining a Decentralized Future

Bitcoin, blockchain, Ethereum, DeFi, and Web3 are all technologies that have the potential to shape the future in significant ways. In this chapter, we will explore the potential of these technologies and imagine what a decentralized future might look like.

Bitcoin is a decentralized digital currency that uses cryptography to secure financial transactions. The most significant potential of Bitcoin is its ability to function as a global, peer-to-peer payment network without the need for a central authority. This means that individuals can send and receive money from anyone, anywhere in the world, without having to go through a bank or other financial institution.

Blockchain is a distributed ledger technology that allows multiple parties to record and verify transactions without the need for a central authority. It was first implemented as the underlying technology for Bitcoin, but it has since been used for a variety of other purposes.

The potential of blockchain lies in its ability to create trust between parties that may not know each other and to create a secure and transparent record of transactions.

Ethereum is an open-source, decentralized platform that runs smart contracts: applications that run exactly as programmed without any possibility of downtime, censorship, fraud, or third-party interference. Ethereum was created in 2015 by Vitalik Buterin and has since become one of the most popular platforms for decentralized applications (dApps).

The potential of Ethereum lies in its ability to enable the creation of decentralized, autonomous organizations (DAOs) and to facilitate the creation of decentralized finance (DeFi) applications.

DeFi refers to a new financial system that is built on top of blockchain technology. It enables the creation of decentralized financial instruments such as loans, savings accounts, and insurance policies that are transparent, secure, and accessible to anyone with an internet connection. DeFi has the potential to create financial inclusion for people who may not have access to traditional financial services and to create more efficient financial markets.

Web3 refers to the next generation of the internet that is being built on top of decentralized technologies such as blockchain and peer-to-peer networking. It has the potential to create a more decentralized, secure, and transparent internet that is less reliant on centralized entities such as large tech companies and governments.
So what might a decentralized future look like? It is difficult to predict exactly what the future will hold, but some possibilities include:

- A global, peer-to-peer payment network enabled by Bitcoin and other cryptocurrencies. This could lead to faster, cheaper, and more secure financial transactions, and it could enable people in countries with unstable economies or oppressive governments to store and transfer value more easily.
- A decentralized internet enabled by Web3 technologies. This could create a more open

and equitable internet that is less controlled by large tech companies and governments. It could also enable the creation of new types of applications and services that are not possible on the current internet.

- A decentralized financial system enabled by DeFi. This could create more financial inclusion and more efficient financial markets, and it could enable people to access a wider range of financial products and services.

- The emergence of decentralized, autonomous organizations enabled by Ethereum and other blockchain platforms. These organizations could operate without the need for a central authority and could potentially disrupt traditional business models.

Of course, these technologies also have their challenges and limitations. Bitcoin and other cryptocurrencies are still relatively new and are subject to high price volatility. Blockchain technology is still in the early stages of development and has scalability and performance issues. Ethereum and other smart contract platforms have experienced security vulnerabilities and have limited programming languages and resources. DeFi is still in the early stages of development and is subject to regulatory uncertainty and Web3 technologies.

"Cryptocurrency is the future of finance. It enables people to take control of their own wealth and transact directly with one another, without the need for intermediaries."

- Andreas Antonopoulos, author and Bitcoin expert

Chapter 13

Tokenization and the Impact on the Financial Markets.

Tokenization is the process of converting traditional financial assets into digital tokens that can be traded on a blockchain or other distributed ledger technology (DLT). These digital tokens represent ownership of the underlying asset, and can be bought, sold, and traded on digital asset exchanges in a similar way to traditional securities.

Tokenization has the potential to revolutionize traditional financial markets by increasing efficiency, reducing costs, and improving accessibility for investors.

One of the main benefits of tokenization is the ability to fractionalize assets. This means that investors can buy and sell small fractions of an asset, rather than having to purchase the entire asset outright. For example, an investor may only be able to afford a small fraction of a high-value asset, such as a rare artwork or a luxury property.

Tokenization allows these investors to participate in the ownership of these assets by buying a digital token that represents a fraction of the asset. This opens up the possibility for a wider range of investors to participate in the ownership of these assets, increasing liquidity and potentially driving up prices.

Tokenization can also increase the efficiency of trading and settlement processes. Traditional financial markets often involve complex and time-consuming processes for buying and selling assets, including the need for intermediaries such as brokers and clearing houses.

Tokenization allows these processes to be automated using smart contracts, which can facilitate the transfer of ownership and reduce the need for manual intervention. This can help to reduce transaction costs and increase the speed of trades.

In addition to improving efficiency, tokenization can also increase the accessibility of financial markets to a wider range of investors. Traditional financial markets can be difficult for some investors to access, due to high barriers to entry such as large minimum investment amounts and complex regulatory requirements.

Tokenization allows investors to participate in financial markets using digital assets, which can be bought and sold with smaller amounts of money and with fewer regulatory barriers. This can help to democratize financial markets and increase participation from a wider range of investors.

Tokenization can also help to reduce the risk of fraud and counterfeiting in financial markets. Digital tokens can be easily verified and tracked on a blockchain, making it difficult for fraudsters to create fake tokens or manipulate the ownership of assets. This can help to increase trust in financial markets and reduce the risk of financial crimes.

There are several different types of assets that can be tokenized, including real estate, artwork, and even traditional securities such as stocks and bonds. Many companies are exploring the use of tokenization to revolutionize traditional financial markets and increase the accessibility and efficiency of trading.

One example of a company using tokenization in the financial market is RealT, which is using tokenization to enable the fractional ownership of real estate assets. Investors can purchase digital tokens that represent ownership of a fraction of a property, and can then trade these tokens on a digital asset exchange. This allows investors to participate in the ownership of high-value real estate assets without having to purchase the entire property outright.

Another example is the tokenization of artworks, which is being explored by companies such as Maecenas and Codex. These companies are using tokenization to enable the fractional ownership of artworks, allowing investors to purchase digital tokens that represent a fraction of the ownership of a piece of art. This allows investors to participate in the ownership of valuable artworks without having to purchase the entire piece outright.

Overall, tokenization has the potential to transform traditional financial markets by increasing efficiency, reducing costs, and improving accessibility for investors. While there are still regulatory hurdles to overcome and challenges to be addressed, the use of tokenization in financial markets is likely to continue to grow and evolve in the coming years.

"Cryptocurrency has the power to democratize finance and bring economic opportunity to anyone with an internet connection."

- Brian Armstrong, CEO of Coinbase

Chapter 14

Centralized Exchanges versus Decentralize
Exchanges: Are they all Equal.

Cryptocurrencies and blockchain
technology have revolutionized the way we think
about financial transactions and the exchange of
value. While traditional financial systems rely on
central entities to facilitate and regulate
exchanges, cryptocurrencies have introduced the
concept of decentralized exchanges, or DEXes,
which operate without a central authority.

On the other hand, centralized exchanges,
or CEXes, have a central point of control and are
operated by a single entity or group. These
exchanges are more common and have been
around longer than DEXes. They offer a range of
services, including buying and selling
cryptocurrencies, storing and safeguarding assets,
and facilitating transactions between parties.

So, what are the main differences between
CEXes and DEXes, and which one is right for you?

Here are some key points to consider:

1. Decentralization: As mentioned, the main difference between CEXes and DEXes is the level of decentralization. CEXes are controlled by a central authority, while DEXes operate on a decentralized network. This means that DEXes do not have a single point of control or failure, and transactions are processed directly between users without the need for intermediaries. This can provide a higher level of security and privacy for users, as there is no central entity holding and potentially misusing user data.

2. Security: Both CEXes and DEXes have their own security risks, and it's important to do your research and understand the specific security measures in place before choosing an exchange. That being said, DEXes can offer a higher level of security due to their decentralized nature. Since there is no central point of control, it is more difficult for hackers to target and potentially compromise the exchange. CEXes, on the other hand, have been the target of numerous high-profile hacks in the past, leading to the loss of significant amounts of user assets.

3. Liquidity: One of the main advantages of CEXes is the high liquidity they offer. As they are more established and widely used, CEXes typically have a larger pool of users and a greater volume of trades, making it easier to buy and sell cryptocurrencies at a fair market price. DEXes, on the other hand, tend to have lower liquidity due to their smaller user base and less widespread adoption. This can make it more difficult to buy and sell large amounts of cryptocurrencies on DEXes, as there may not be enough buyers or sellers to match your trade.

4. Fees: Both CEXes and DEXes charge fees for their services, but the types and amount of fees can vary significantly. CEXes often charge higher fees than DEXes, as they offer a wider range of services and have to cover the costs of maintaining and operating their central infrastructure. DEXes, on the other hand, tend to have lower fees due to their decentralized nature and the lack of a central entity to cover costs. However, it's important to keep in mind that DEXes may also charge other

fees, such as gas fees for processing transactions on the blockchain.

5. Regulation: CEXes are more likely to be regulated by financial authorities, as they operate as traditional financial institutions. This means that they may be subject to stricter regulations and oversight, which can provide a higher level of security and protection for users. DEXes, on the other hand, are not subject to the same level of regulation due to their decentralized nature. This can be both an advantage and a disadvantage, as it allows for greater freedom and autonomy, but also means that users may not have the same level of protection if something goes wrong.

"Cryptocurrency is going to change the world, and those who embrace it early on will be the ones who reap the biggest rewards."

- Tim Draper, venture capitalist

Chapter 15

Trading Cryptocurrencies: a Scary Risky Business

Trading cryptocurrencies can be a risky endeavor for a number of reasons. Here are some of the main risks to consider before diving into the world of cryptocurrency trading:

1. Volatility: One of the most well-known risks of trading cryptocurrencies is their high level of volatility. Cryptocurrencies are known for their rapid price movements, which can result in significant losses for traders who are unprepared for the risks. For example, the price of Bitcoin, the most well-known cryptocurrency, has been known to swing by hundreds or even thousands of dollars in a single day. This volatility can make it difficult for traders to predict the direction of the market, making it difficult to make informed decisions about when to buy and sell.

2. Lack of regulation: Another risk of trading cryptocurrencies is the lack of regulation in

the market. Unlike traditional financial markets, which are regulated by governments and financial institutions, the cryptocurrency market is largely unregulated. This means that there is no central authority overseeing the market, which can make it more prone to fraud and manipulation. For example, there have been instances of cryptocurrency exchanges being hacked and investors losing their funds. There is also a risk of fraudsters creating fake cryptocurrencies or initial coin offerings (ICOs) in order to defraud investors.

3. Lack of liquidity: Another risk of trading cryptocurrencies is the lack of liquidity in the market. While some cryptocurrencies, like Bitcoin, have relatively high levels of liquidity, others may have much lower liquidity. This means that it may be difficult for traders to buy or sell large amounts of certain cryptocurrencies without significantly affecting the price. This can make it difficult for traders to enter or exit positions in the market, which can be a significant risk for those who are not prepared for it.

4. Security risks: Trading cryptocurrencies also carries security risks, as there have been instances of exchanges being hacked and investors losing their funds. It is important for traders to take steps to protect their cryptocurrency assets, such as using strong passwords, enabling two-factor authentication, and storing their assets in a secure wallet.

5. Limited adoption: Despite the growing popularity of cryptocurrencies, they are still not widely accepted as a form of payment, which can limit their utility. This means that traders may have difficulty finding merchants who are willing to accept cryptocurrencies, which can make it difficult to turn their investments into cash.

6. Technical challenges: Trading cryptocurrencies can also be challenging for those who are not familiar with the technical aspects of the market. For example, traders may need to navigate complex trading platforms and understand technical terms like "blockchain" and

"mining." This can be a barrier for those who are not familiar with the technology, which can be a significant risk for those who are new to the market.

7. Market manipulation: As mentioned earlier, the lack of regulation in the cryptocurrency market can make it more susceptible to market manipulation. There have been instances of traders using tactics like "pump and dump" schemes to artificially inflate the price of certain cryptocurrencies, only to sell off their holdings and profit from the price increase. This can be a significant risk for traders who are not aware of these tactics and can result in significant losses.

In conclusion, trading cryptocurrencies can be very risky due to their high level of volatility, lack of regulation, lack of liquidity, security risks, limited adoption, and potential for market manipulation. It is important for traders to carefully consider these risks before entering the market and to take steps to protect themselves and their investments. This may include educating themselves about the market and the specific cryptocurrencies they are interested in trading, diversifying their portfolio, and working with a trusted financial advisor or professional.

"You have to be bullish if you believe in crypto regulation"

- Kevin O'Leary, TV Personality

Chapter 16

Rules and Regulations of Cryptocurrencies:
To be or not to be

Cryptocurrencies are digital or virtual currencies that use cryptography for secure financial transactions and to verify the transfer of assets. They operate on a decentralized network, meaning they are not controlled by any government or financial institution.

Since the creation of the first cryptocurrency, Bitcoin, in 2009, the use of cryptocurrencies has grown significantly.

However, the lack of regulation in this area has led to some concerns about their potential use for illegal activities and the lack of protection for consumers.

As a result, many countries have started to introduce rules and regulations for cryptocurrencies to address these concerns and provide a framework for the use of these digital assets.

One of the main issues with cryptocurrencies is their potential use for money laundering and other illegal activities. To address this, many countries have introduced Know Your Customer (KYC) and Anti-Money Laundering (AML) regulations for cryptocurrency exchanges and other service providers.

These regulations require exchanges and other service providers to verify the identity of their customers and report any suspicious activity to the relevant authorities.

Another issue with cryptocurrencies is their volatility, which makes them a risky investment. To protect consumers, some countries have introduced regulations that require exchanges to hold a certain amount of capital to cover any potential losses.

In addition to these specific regulations, some countries have also introduced more general rules and regulations for cryptocurrencies. For example, the United States has issued guidance on how to treat cryptocurrencies for tax purposes, and the Internal Revenue Service (IRS) has issued guidance on the reporting of cryptocurrency transactions.

In Europe, the European Banking Authority (EBA) has issued guidelines on the risks associated with cryptocurrencies and has recommended that national regulators take a risk-based approach to regulating them.

Many countries have also introduced specific regulations for Initial Coin Offerings (ICOs), which are a form of crowdfunding using cryptocurrencies. These regulations often require companies to disclose information about the ICO, including the use of funds and the risk involved, to protect investors.

Despite these efforts, the regulation of cryptocurrencies remains a challenging and evolving area. Some countries, such as Japan and Switzerland, have taken a more permissive approach to cryptocurrencies and have established a legal framework for their use. Other countries, such as China and India, have taken a more restrictive approach and have banned or limited the use of cryptocurrencies.

Overall, the rules and regulations on cryptocurrencies vary significantly from country to country. As the use of cryptocurrencies continues to grow, it is likely that more countries will introduce specific regulations to address the risks and concerns associated with these digital assets.

"Don't steal, the Government hates competition"

- Ron Paul, retired U.S. Representative for Texas

Chapter 17

The Rise and Fall of Crypto: The Good, the
Bad and the Ugly

The crypto industry, or cryptocurrency industry, is a relatively new and rapidly growing sector that has gained significant attention in recent years. It refers to the use of digital or virtual currencies, such as bitcoin and Ethereum, as a means of exchange or as a store of value.

These digital currencies are decentralized, meaning they are not controlled by any government or financial institution. Instead, they rely on complex algorithms and a decentralized network of computers to verify and validate transactions.

One of the biggest successes of the crypto industry has been the emergence of bitcoin as a legitimate and widely recognized digital currency. Bitcoin was the first cryptocurrency to be created, and it has since gained widespread acceptance and adoption. In the early days, bitcoin was primarily used for illicit purposes, such as buying drugs on the dark web. However, as the cryptocurrency has become more mainstream, it has been accepted by a growing number of merchants and online platforms as a legitimate form of payment.

Another major success of the crypto industry has been the emergence of initial coin offerings (ICOs). ICOs are a way for companies to raise funds by issuing their own digital tokens, which are typically built on top of an existing blockchain platform such as Ethereum. Many companies have successfully raised millions of dollars through ICOs, and this has helped to fuel the growth of the crypto industry.

However, the crypto industry has also been plagued by scams and fraudulent activities. One of the most notorious examples of this is the collapse of the Mt. Gox exchange in 2014. Mt. Gox was one of the largest bitcoin exchanges at the time, but it suffered a major hack that resulted in the theft of 850,000 bitcoins, worth around $450 million at the time. The hack and subsequent collapse of Mt. Gox had a significant impact on the crypto industry, and it took years for bitcoin to recover from the damage.

Another major scam in the crypto industry was the OneCoin Ponzi scheme. OneCoin claimed to be a legitimate cryptocurrency, but it was actually a

Ponzi scheme that defrauded investors out of millions of dollars. The founders of OneCoin were eventually arrested and charged with fraud.

Other scams in the crypto industry have included Ponzi schemes, pyramid schemes, and fake ICOs that promised high returns but ultimately failed to deliver. These scams have often targeted inexperienced investors who were lured in by the hype and promise of easy profits.

Most recently the rise and fall of FTX, a Centralized Exchange and the arrest of its founder Sam Bankman-Fried, who is awaiting trial charged with several counts of fraud.

In conclusion, the crypto industry has experienced both significant successes and scams over the past decade. While the emergence of bitcoin and the growth of ICOs have helped to legitimize the industry, it has also been plagued by fraudulent activities and scams that have harmed investors and damaged the reputation of the sector. It is important for investors to be cautious and do their due diligence before investing in any cryptocurrency or ICO, as the risks and uncertainties associated with these investments are high.

Conclusion

In conclusion, Bitcoin, blockchain, smart contracts, and exchanges have revolutionized the way we think about and use technology in the financial sector. Bitcoin, the first and most well-known cryptocurrency, has garnered significant attention due to its decentralized nature and potential to disrupt traditional financial systems.

Blockchain, the underlying technology behind Bitcoin, has also gained traction in various industries due to its ability to securely and transparently record transactions. Smart contracts, self-executing contracts with the terms of the agreement between buyer and seller being directly written into lines of code, have the potential to revolutionize the way we do business by automating and streamlining legal processes.

Exchanges, platforms where individuals can buy and sell cryptocurrencies, have made it easier for people to access and participate in the cryptocurrency market. However, it's important to note that the cryptocurrency market is highly volatile and carries a high level of risk. It's crucial for individuals to thoroughly research and understand the risks before investing in cryptocurrency.

Despite the potential and hype surrounding these technologies, it's important to recognize that they are still in the early stages of development and adoption. There are still numerous challenges and uncertainties that need to be addressed, such as regulation, security, and scalability.

Overall, the future of Bitcoin, blockchain, smart contracts, and exchanges is uncertain, but the impact they have already had on the financial industry and beyond is undeniable. As these technologies continue to evolve and mature, it will be interesting to see how they shape and change the way we interact with and use technology in the future.

Appendix 1

Here are websites that provide information about bitcoin, blockchain, smart contracts, pricing of cryptocurrencies, and crypto exchanges:

1. Bitcoin.org - Provides information about bitcoin and its history, as well as resources for developers.

2. Blockchain.com - A popular website for tracking and managing bitcoin transactions, as well as buying and selling bitcoin.

3. Ethereum.org - The website for the Ethereum blockchain, which is a popular platform for building smart contracts.

4. CoinMarketCap - A website that tracks the prices of various cryptocurrencies and provides market data.

5. CoinDesk - A news and information website focused on bitcoin and other cryptocurrencies.

6. CryptoCompare - A website that allows users to compare the prices and features of various cryptocurrencies and crypto exchanges.

7. BitcoinTalk - An online forum for discussing bitcoin and other cryptocurrencies.

8. Reddit - A popular social news and discussion website that has a number of subreddit communities devoted to bitcoin and other cryptocurrencies.

9. CoinTelegraph - A news and information website focused on bitcoin and other cryptocurrencies.

10. Bitcointalk.org - An online forum for discussing bitcoin and other cryptocurrencies.

Appendix 2

- Binance
- Coinbase
- Kraken
- Bitfinex
- Bitstamp
- Bittrex
- CEX.io
- Huobi
- Fortaleza Digital
- OKEx

It's worth noting that the specific exchanges that are the best for you may depend on your location, the cryptocurrencies you want to trade, and your personal trading style. It's always a good idea to do your own research and compare the fees, security measures, and available cryptocurrencies on multiple exchanges before deciding which one is the best fit for you.

Additionally, it's important to remember to never store large amounts of cryptocurrency on an exchange, as exchanges can be vulnerable to hacking and other security threats. Instead, it's generally recommended to store your cryptocurrency in a secure wallet.

CPSIA information can be obtained
at www.ICGtesting.com
Printed in the USA
LVHW081931300123
738245LV00029B/1124

9 781387 389575